ISN'T IT ROMANTIC

ISN'T IT ROMANTIC

Nat Segaloff
and
Daniel M. Kimmel

LONGMEADOW
PRESS

Cover and interior design by Barbara Cohen Aronica

Cover photo: Intermezzo, 1939

ISBN 0-681-41402-2

Printed in Singapore

First Edition

0 9 8 7 6 5 4 3 2 1

DEDICATIONS

To Ruth and Bertram Segaloff, who loved each other.
—N.S.

To Donna, for the best love story of all.
—D.K.

PHOTO CREDITS

Columbia Pictures
David O. Selznick Productions
Metro-Goldwyn-Mayer
Paramount Pictures
The Rank Organisation
RKO Radio Pictures
Samuel Goldwyn Productions
Twentieth Century-Fox
United Artists
Universal Pictures
Warner Bros.

Contents

ISN'T IT ROMANTIC

Brief Encounter *(1945)*

For most lovers, a romance is an eruption of great passion. For some, though—such as those who happen to be already married—the joys of an affair dare not be spoken aloud. This is the exquisite mood of *Brief Encounter*, the quiet story of unconsummated love between a middle-class doctor (Trevor Howard) and a housewife (Celia Johnson). If anything disproves the myth that the British are poor lovers, it is this restrained, yet extraordinarily affecting, motion picture.

In its skillful contrasting of supercharged situations with underplayed performances, *Brief Encounter* is the greatest romance to come out of England since Edward VIII gave up the throne for the women he loved.

DIRECTOR: *David Lean*
WITH: *Celia Johnson, Trevor Howard*

Camille *(1936)*

The unabashedly romantic *Camille* had already been filmed no fewer than six times before Greta Garbo starred as Alexandre Dumas *fils*' tragic "Lady of the Camellias." Set in the Paris of 1847, the story follows the fated liaison of young Armand Duvall (Robert Taylor) and Marguerite Gauthier (Greta Garbo), a scintillating and magnetically beautiful courtesan.

Most people remember *Camille*, despite its lighter moments, for the tears it brings. In part, these tears are shed for lost innocence. Like our first true love, the fond recollection of which secretly sustains us for a lifetime, *Camille* is a flower pressed between the pages of a diary, a keepsake that lives only in that soft-focus memory we accord a cherished movie.

DIRECTOR: George Cukor
WITH: Greta Garbo, Robert Taylor, Lionel Barrymore

Casablanca (1942)

When Ingrid Bergman was making *Casablanca* she had a problem: Was her character, Ilsa Lund, supposed to end up with her lover, Rick (Humphrey Bogart), or return to her husband, Victor Laszlo (Paul Henreid)? Until they shot the ending of the film, nobody knew for sure. As a result, when Ilsa appears confused over what to do ("You'll have to think for both of us," she tells Rick) Bergman was being utterly sincere.

Supposedly two endings were written, one with Ilsa going off with Victor and one with her remaining behind with Rick. After shooting the first ending, the filmmakers realized that there was no need for the alternative. Perhaps the best explanation for the film's endless appeal is that it stands for a love being so grand that one is willing to sacrifice it for something even greater.

DIRECTOR: Michael Curtiz
WITH: Humphrey Bogart, Ingrid Bergman, Paul Henreid, Claude Rains, Conrad Veidt, Dooley Wilson, Sydney Greenstreet, Peter Lorre, S. Z. Sakall

The Clock (1945)

The clock in the title of this Vincente Minnelli drama has both an actual and symbolic meaning. Literally, it is the clock at the Astor Hotel, under which Manhattan secretary Alice Mayberry (Judy Garland) and Corporal Joe Allen (Robert Walker) have agreed to meet for a date. Figuratively, it represents the pressure of time: within forty-eight hours they meet, fall in love, get married, and part.

The final scene shows Joe and Alice parting at the train station, with other wives seeing other husbands off to war. As Alice leaves, Minnelli's camera pulls up and away so that Alice blends into the swirling crowd around her. There are love stories all around us, he is saying, if we only know to stop and look.

In one sense, Minnelli was right about the possibility of romance being right under one's nose. After he finished filming *The Clock*, he married Garland.

DIRECTOR: Vincente Minnelli
WITH: Judy Garland, Robert Walker, James Gleason, Keenan Wynn

Doctor Zhivago *(1965)*

Swooning over its snowy vistas, sighing with its secret lovers, or humming along with "Lara's Theme," for nearly three decades moviegoers have fallen under the spell of *Doctor Zhivago*. Its sprawling story focuses on the adulterous romance between an aristocratic doctor-poet (Omar Sharif) and a young revolutionary (Julie Christie), while catching audiences in the sweep of the Russian revolution as well as the travails of its complex characters. The film offered its meticulous director, David Lean, an immense stage on which to play out, as the ads promised, "a love caught in the fire of revolution."

DIRECTOR: *David Lean*
WITH: *Omar Sharif, Julie Christie, Rod Steiger, Geraldine Chaplin*

The Enchanted Cottage *(1945)*

The Enchanted Cottage is such a discovery that many of its fans sincerely believe they are the only ones who know of it. In happy fact, it is a favorite of millions. Robert Young plays a disfigured World War II flyer whose love for a homely young woman, Dorothy McGuire, makes them appear beautiful to each other. Outsiders, of course, know the truth, but sensing the purity of their love encourage the fantasy.

The Enchanted Cottage is based on benign deception; it works only because the audience assists in the fantasy. This very naiveté is what makes this fragile story so endearing. Like a twist on Dante's vision, the sign above the door of the enchanted cottage should read, "*Embrace* all faith, ye who enter here."

DIRECTOR: *John Cromwell*
WITH: *Robert Young, Dorothy McGuire, Herbert Marshall*

The Gay Divorcée *(1934)*

When one talks of romantic musical comedy there is Astaire and Rogers, and then there is everyone else. In the 1930s they were the premiere musical comedy team, so associated with each other that when their series of films ended it seemed as if an era had drawn to a close. And indeed it had.

In the world of an Astaire-Rogers film, there is only one suitable time for romance, and that is while dancing. When Astaire professes his love for Rogers in "Night and Day," what follows is a dance sequence that transforms the character from comical combatants to lovers. First Astaire is a supplicant, pleading with Rogers to remain. Finally, they dance together in joyful celebration twirling around cheek to cheek; the whole number is one of seduction and consummation. At the conclusion of the dance Rogers sits languidly on a couch and Astaire offers: "Cigarette?"

DIRECTOR: *Mark Sandrich*
WITH: *Fred Astaire, Ginger Rogers, Edward Everett Horton, Alice Brady, Eric Blore, Erik Rhodes*

Gone With the Wind (*1939*)

If ever a single motion picture embodied all the passion, the drama, the skill, and the mythmaking of Hollywood at the apex of its power, that motion picture is *Gone With the Wind*.

Now part of Americana, *Gone With the Wind* is the extraordinary epic of Scarlett O'Hara and her husbands Charles Hamilton (Rand Brooks), Frank Kennedy (Carroll Nye) and Rhett Butler (Clark Gable), as well as her undying, unrequited, love for Ashley Wilkes (Leslie Howard). But most of all, Scarlett loves Tara, her home. It hardly matters that all of them are doomed; as long as we continue to hope otherwise, *Gone With the Wind* will remain as resilient as Katie Scarlett O'Hara, the red earth of Georgia, and Tara itself.

DIRECTOR: Victor Fleming
WITH: Clark Gable, Vivien Leigh, Leslie Howard

The Goodbye Girl (1977)

Some filmmakers have found love in New York's slums (*West Side Story*), others in its glitzy skyscrapers (*Manhattan*), and others under the Brooklyn Bridge (*Moonstruck*). But in *The Goodbye Girl*, Neil Simon has found it in a rent-controlled midtown apartment.

Marsha Mason (Simon's then-wife) is the oft-jilted woman who is forced to share quarters with the glib Richard Dreyfuss. After some early sparring, they are united not only in love but in their concern for Mason's daughter (Quinn Cummings), whose precocious behavior helps draw them all together into a family.

The Goodbye Girl is about people who lower their guard long enough to see the kindness in each other. It's also a snazzy love letter to New York and happy proof that Hollywood *can* "make them like they used to."

DIRECTOR: *Herbert Ross*
WITH: *Richard Dreyfuss, Marsha Mason, Quinn Cummings*

Holiday (*1 9 3 8*)

In *Holiday*, Johnny Case (Cary Grant) finds his ideal woman. Unfortunately for him, it is his fiancée's sister. On a brief holiday ski trip he meets the lovely Julia Seton (Doris Nolan), who he thinks will be "the perfect playmate." Yet what Julia really wants is for him to concentrate on accumulating wealth, as her family has done.

Her sister, Linda (Katharine Hepburn), loathes the family's life-style and finds herself falling in love with Johnny. It's an awkward triangle, since Linda doesn't want to compete with Julia. She tries everything she can to keep them together but, in the end, Johnny breaks it off.

In one of the great romantic clinches, Cary Grant is doing his trademark backflip when Linda arrives. As he falls to the floor, she kneels down to join him and we know that Johnny has found his "perfect playmate" at last.

DIRECTOR: *George Cukor*
WITH: *Cary Grant, Katharine Hepburn, Lew Ayres, Henry Kolker, Doris Nolan, Jean Dixon, Edward Everett Horton, Henry Daniell, Binnie Barnes*

It Happened One Night (1934)

Spoiled heiress Ellie Andrews (Claudette Colbert) is fleeing from her father (Walter Connolly), who is getting her spur-of-the-moment marriage annulled. Peter Warne (Clark Gable) is the unemployed reporter who promises to get her back to her husband if he can get the exclusive story. Along the way, these two strong-willed characters end up falling in love with each other.

Director Frank Capra and writer Robert Riskin helped establish the "screwball" romances of the 1930s, letting the romantic leads handle the comedy instead of casting established comedians. Ironically, this now-classic movie was initially looked on as punishment by its two stars, who didn't know they were making history. The finished film enhanced the careers of virtually everyone associated with it and became one of only two pictures to win all five top Oscars: Best Picture, Best Director, Best Screenplay, Best Actor, and Best Actress.

DIRECTOR: Frank Capra
WITH: Clark Gable, Claudette Colbert, Walter Connolly, Roscoe Karns, Alan Hale

Love Affair *(1939)*

Overshadowed by its better-known remake (*An Affair to Remember*, 1957), the more skillful *Love Affair* is both funny and dramatic: a story of a romance so great that it survives tragedy.

Charles Boyer and Irene Dunne star as the playboy and the "good woman" who meet on board a ship, pledge their hearts, and then suffer endlessly when each mistakenly thinks the other has ditched him.

Love Affair may sound improbable, but it is a complex and original work—an endearing story of unqualified love as well as a moving and enduring screen memory.

DIRECTOR: *Leo McCarey*
WITH: *Charles Boyer, Irene Dunne*

L o v e   S t o r y *(1 9 7 0)*

As an over-the-top celebration of tragic love, *Love Story* has no modern equal. Jennifer Cavilleri (Ali MacGraw) is the poor Italian girl who meets Harvard preppie Oliver Barrett III (Ryan O'Neal). Their parents have varying doubts, the lovers do not; they get married, then she gets sick and dies.

No plot could have been more, well, Hollywood. Yet movie audiences (perhaps hardened by the ultra-reality of Vietnam) embraced it and made *Love Story* a box office phenomenon.

Its success lies in its purity. Jenny and Ollie care deeply about each other and nothing—not parents or logic—dulls their passion. This is a straightforward, no-frills movie that reaches right into the viewer's heart. In the lore of love, nothing else matters.

DIRECTOR: *Arthur Hiller*
WITH: *Ryan O'Neal, Ali MacGraw*

Magnificent Obsession (1954)

Bob Merrick (Rock Hudson) is a medical school dropout who inadvertently causes the death of a saintly doctor. The widow, Helen Phillips (Jane Wyman), doubts she can ever forgive him. Bob tries to make amends when he sees her at a restaurant, but when she attempts to flee she is struck by a car and blinded.

Humiliated, Bob decides to return to medical school and become a surgeon. Without revealing his true identity, he also begins romancing the sightless Helen, hoping to earn her love. Then she becomes seriously ill. An operation can save her life *and* restore her sight, but it must be performed immediately. The only surgeon in the facility at that very moment is none other than Bob, whose "magnificent obsession" has given him the opportunity to undo all the wrong he has done, and be worthy of Helen at last.

Hokey as it sounds, *Magnificent Obsession* works because it never loses sight of its belief in the redemptive power of love.

DIRECTOR: *Douglas Sirk*
WITH: *Jane Wyman, Rock Hudson, Agnes Moorehead, Otto Kruger*

My Man Godfrey *(1936)*

My Man Godfrey is the answer to what happens when an immovable object meets an irresistible force: Something's got to give. The immovable object is Godfrey (William Powell), a surprisingly erudite derelict who lives in a riverside dump near a posh Manhattan neighborhood. The irresistible force is Irene Bullock (Carole Lombard), a scatterbrained heiress who always knows what *she's* doing and can't understand when other people can't keep up.

The chemistry here between Powell and Lombard is especially interesting when one remembers that they had been married and had divorced a few years earlier. They did remain friends, and when he was loaned by MGM to Universal Pictures for *My Man Godfrey* Powell, ever the gentleman, insisted that the part of Irene go to his ex-wife.

DIRECTOR: Gregory La Cava
WITH: William Powell, Carole Lombard, Gail Patrick, Eugene Pallette, Alice Brady, Mischa Auer

North By Northwest *(1959)*

Alfred Hitchcock's classic comedy-thriller asks you to check your disbelief at the door: Twice-divorced ad executive Roger O. Thornhill (Cary Grant) finds himself mistaken for CIA agent George Kaplan *and* wanted for murder. Roger's salvation will come through meeting the beautiful Eve Kendall (Eva Marie Saint) aboard a Chicago-bound train and learning to care for the fate of someone other than himself.

Roger's adventures constitute a turning away from the thoughtlessness and glibness that have characterized his existence up until this point. "My wives divorced me," he tells Eve during the climactic chase over Mount Rushmore. "I think they said I led too dull a life."

It is while hanging from atop the monument that they must work together and literally reach out for each other. As Thornhill pulls Eve to safety, the scene dissolves to a cabin on a train, where he is pulling her into the berth they will share. She is now the latest—and presumably the last—Mrs. Thornhill.

DIRECTOR: *Alfred Hitchcock*
WITH: *Cary Grant, Eva Marie Saint, James Mason, Martin Landau, Leo G. Carroll, Jessie Royce Landis, Edward Platt*

Picnic *(1955)*

In *Picnic*, most of the characters see love as the magic tonic that will solve their problems. Hal (William Holden) drifts into town on Labor Day and meets Madge (Kim Novak). They come together during the film's big moment—their dance after Madge has been crowned Queen of Neewollah ("Halloween" spelled backwards).

Everyone is breathless as they watch Hal and Madge make beautiful music together. Their love enables them to break out of their shells, so when Hal is forced to flee town, Madge has the courage to pick herself up and leave as well. Both feel inadequate, yet each reaches out to help the other. If there is redemption to be found in romance, *Picnic* tells us it is in those moments of reaching out.

DIRECTOR: *Joshua Logan*
WITH:*William Holden, Kim Novak, Rosalind Russell, Arthur O'Connell, Cliff Robertson, Susan Strasberg*

Romeo and Juliet *(1968)*

Star-crossed lovers have always been a good subject for romance, but *young* star-crossed lovers such as Romeo and Juliet are special. As Leonard Whiting and Olivia Hussey exuberantly demonstrate in Franco Zeffirelli's 1968 version of Shakespeare's classic, nothing can stop the zeal and passion of teenagers.

Little in *Romeo and Juliet* could have been familiar to the millions of dating couples who proclaimed it their "special" film. The dresses were old-fashioned, the language was remote, the morals were positively archaic, and the hero wore *tights*!

But when boy meets girl, the centuries dissolve—and with them the audience. Zeffirelli has made other love stories (*Endless Love*, 1981) and directed other Shakespeare (*The Taming of the Shrew*, 1967; *Hamlet*, 1990), but none has the durable appeal of this most innocent and energetic romance.

DIRECTOR: *Franco Zeffirelli*
WITH: *Leonard Whiting, Olivia Hussey*

South Pacific *(1958)*

South Pacific has all the elements of a lush cruise aboard the "Love Boat," plus music and a social conscience. Set during World War II, it focuses on two interracial romances—one between the white Lieutenant Cable (John Kerr) and the Polynesian Liat (France Nuyen), the other between nurse Nellie Forbush (Mitzi Gaynor) and widower Emile de Becque (Rossano Brazzi), who had fathered children by a native girl.

As the film powerfully argues, with the whole world at war, why should people be torn apart by prejudice? Like the mystical, mythical island of Bali H'ai that tempts the sailors, *South Pacific* tempts audiences to pine for something that is as far away as perfection, yet as close as the desire to attain it.

DIRECTOR: *Joshua Logan*
WITH: *Rossano Brazzi, Mitzi Gaynor, John Kerr, France Nuyen*

The Thin Man (1934)

This mystery-comedy series, based on the popular novel by Dashiell Hammett, showed that fun and romance don't have to end after the wedding bells stop ringing. Unlike the lovers in most romantic comedies, the *Thin Man* movies didn't have to rely on Nick and Nora Charles (William Powell and Myrna Loy) making or renewing their vows. Apparently, the couple that solves murders together, stays together.

Nick's raffish charm is the perfect complement to Nora's sophisticated wit. When Nick and Nora appeared in their final film—*Song of the Thin Man* (1947)—they had made the transition from being newlyweds to being an old married couple. And they were still very much in love.

DIRECTOR: *W. S. Van Dyke II*
WITH: *William Powell, Myrna Loy, Maureen O'Sullivan, Nat Pendleton, Cesar Romero*

To Have and Have Not *(1945)*

"You know you don't have to act with me, Steve. You don't have to say anything, and you don't have to do anything. Not a thing. Oh, maybe, just whistle. You know how to whistle, don't you, Steve? You just put your lips together and blow."

This scene between Humphrey Bogart and Lauren Bacall has a special place on the short list of the most memorable moments in movie history. Not only is there an obvious chemistry between the characters on-screen, but Bogart and Bacall were igniting sparks off-screen as well. Today, we watch *To Have and Have Not* not because of the story, but because it is one of those rare instances where we know that the romance is the real McCoy.

DIRECTOR: *Howard Hawks*
WITH: *Humphrey Bogart, Lauren Bacall, Walter Brennan, Hoagy Carmichael, Marcel Dalio, Sheldon Leonard*

The Way We Were (1973)

What Robert Redford brings to many of his films are his good looks and the sense that, underneath, he is trying to break free from the limitations placed on him by others because of his physical appearance. Nowhere is that more apparent than in this story of doomed love between Hubbell Gardiner (Redford) and Katie Morosky (Barbra Streisand).

They are attracted by each other's differences, but Katie sees an idealized Hubbell rather than the actual man. "When you love someone," he tells her, "you go deaf, dumb, and blind."

For Robert Redford, *The Way We Were* made him one of the romantic icons of the decade. Barbra Streisand, already a major star since her 1968 Oscar-winning debut in *Funny Girl*, struck a chord with those who had reached for a romantic possibility that was ultimately beyond their grasp.

DIRECTOR: Sydney Pollack
WITH: Barbra Streisand, Robert Redford, Bradford Dillman, James Woods, Lois Chiles, Patrick O'Neal

West Side Story (1961)

Romeo and Juliet inspired *West Side Story*, which pairs the American Tony (Richard Beymer) with the Puerto Rican Maria (Natalie Wood) against the background of warring families—in this case, the gangs of New York's Hell's Kitchen.

Leonard Bernstein's music and Stephen Sondheim's lyrics elevate *West Side Story* above the level of mere romance, making it a swirling, throbbing elegy to young love and the very real forces that seek to crush it. Outstanding supporting performances from Rita Moreno, George Chakiris and Russ Tamblyn combine with those of leads Beymer and Wood to make a moviegoing experience that touches an entire range of emotions.

Arthur Laurents's adaptation of Shakespeare doesn't add a happy ending but it creates a hopeful one which has kept this Oscar-winning film alive for generations of lovers.

DIRECTOR: *Robert Wise, Jerome Robbins*
WITH: *Natalie Wood, Richard Beymer*

Wuthering Heights *(1939)*

Emily Brontë's brooding tale of the Gypsy stable boy, Heathcliff (Laurence Olivier), and his lifelong pursuit of the genteel Cathy (Merle Oberon), who secretly loves but rejects him, is not only one of the most-read books in American schools, it is also one of the most vividly remembered romantic films from Hollywood's Golden Era.

Who can forget Heathcliff and Cathy's idylls in the heather of the Yorkshire Moors? The stormy night when they part? The hesitant eroticism of their reunion? The doom that haunts them to their graves? But most of all, who can resist this evocative gothic fairy tale about a fragile heroine in love with the tall, dark stranger who also happens to be the boy next door?

DIRECTOR: *William Wyler*
WITH: *Laurence Olivier, Merle Oberon*